T0021087

SPACE STATIONS

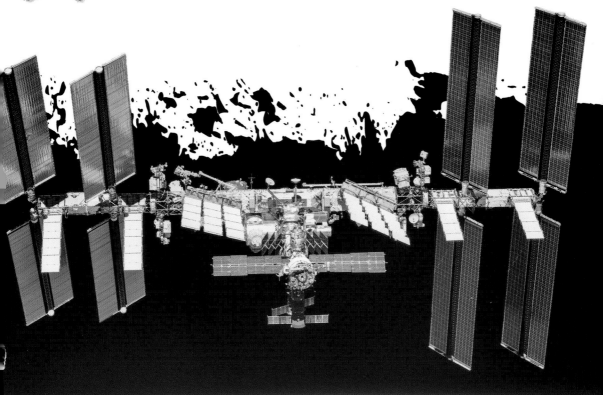

BY DALTON RAINS

Copyright © 2024 by Apex Editions, Mendota Heights, MN 55120. All rights reserved. No part of this book may be reproduced or utilized in any form or by any means without written permission from the publisher.

Apex is distributed by North Star Editions:
sales@northstareditions.com | 888-417-0195

Produced for Apex by Red Line Editorial.

Photographs ©: NASA, cover, 4–5, 6–7, 8–9, 16–17, 18, 19, 20–21, 22–23, 26–27; Roscosmos/NASA, 1, 13; Sovfoto/Universal Images Group/Getty Images, 10–11; F. Carter Smith/Sygma/Getty Images, 12; Liu Fang/Xinhua/AP Images, 15; Daniel J. Rutter/NASA, 24–25, 29

Library of Congress Control Number: 2023910083

ISBN
978-1-63738-742-9 (hardcover)
978-1-63738-785-6 (paperback)
978-1-63738-870-9 (ebook pdf)
978-1-63738-828-0 (hosted ebook)

Printed in the United States of America
Mankato, MN
012024

NOTE TO PARENTS AND EDUCATORS

Apex books are designed to build literacy skills in striving readers. Exciting, high-interest content attracts and holds readers' attention. The text is carefully leveled to allow students to achieve success quickly. Additional features, such as bolded glossary words for difficult terms, help build comprehension.

TABLE OF CONTENTS

CHAPTER 1

SPACEWALK

Two astronauts put on space suits. They are in the International **Space Station** (ISS). The astronauts move into an **airlock**. A door opens, and they climb out. Their spacewalk begins.

In 2019, Jessica Meir (left) and Christina Koch did the first all-female spacewalk.

Astronauts in the ISS can use a large robotic arm for repairs. But sometimes astronauts have to go where the arm cannot reach.

The astronauts float outside the space station. Soon, they reach a long beam called a truss. It carries solar panels.

STAYING SAFE

During spacewalks, astronauts are tethered to the space station. One end of a cable attaches to the astronaut. The other attaches to the station. That way, they do not float away.

Koch and Meir's spacewalk lasted 7 hours and 17 minutes.

The astronauts replace an important device. Then, they return to the airlock. They take off their space suits. Now they can rest.

FAST FACT
Spacewalks often last several hours.

CHAPTER 2

HiSTORY

The **Soviet Union** launched the first space station in 1971. In 1973, the United States launched its own. Astronauts could live on these stations for weeks.

The Soviet Union's Salyut 1 space station circled Earth for 175 days.

Valeri Polyakov did the longest single spaceflight. He spent 437 days on the Mir space station.

In 1986, Russia launched Mir. It was the first **modular** space station. Later, several countries built the ISS. The first part reached **orbit** in 1998. By the 2020s, the ISS had many modules.

MODULES

To build a space station, rockets launch modules. Astronauts and robots put these parts together in space. Some modules are **laboratories**. Others have areas to sleep.

The ISS travels about 17,150 miles per hour (27,600 km/h). It orbits Earth 16 times every day.

In 2021, China launched its own space station. It was called Tiangong. China added two modules to it in 2022.

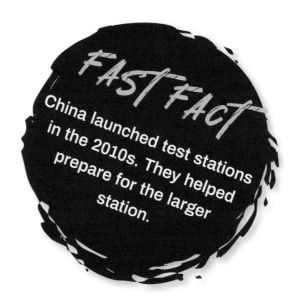

FAST FACT

China launched test stations in the 2010s. They helped prepare for the larger station.

An astronaut works on Tiangong in 2023.

▶

CHAPTER 3

LIFE IN A STATION

Astronauts and supplies enter space stations through **docking ports**. Machines in the station help people breathe. Other machines turn urine into drinking water!

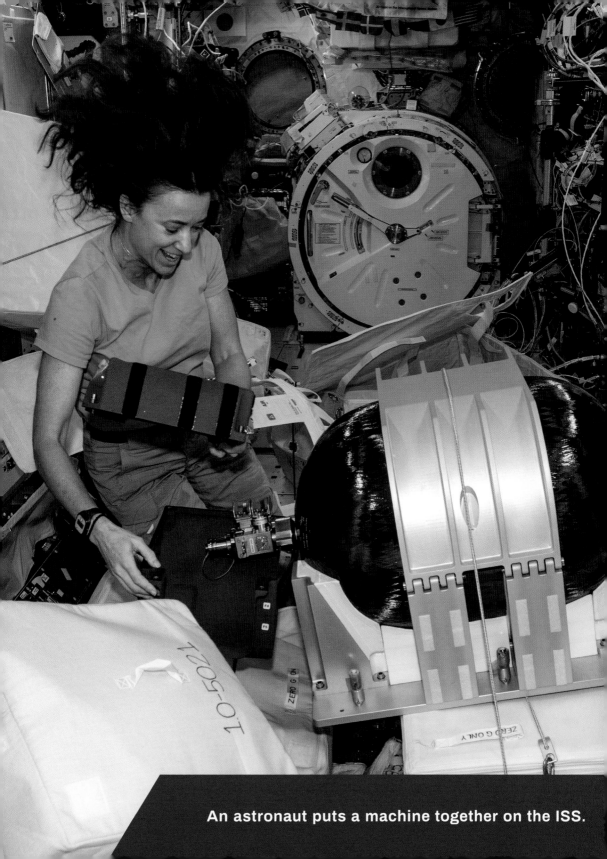

An astronaut puts a machine together on the ISS.

An astronaut stores a science sample in an ISS freezer.

Astronauts do many things
on space stations. They work on
experiments almost every day.
But they also have time to relax.
Some astronauts read books.
Others play or listen to music.

FAST FACT

Muscles can become weak in low gravity. Astronauts exercise two hours every day to stay strong.

Astronauts regularly check their fitness to make sure they are doing enough exercise in space.

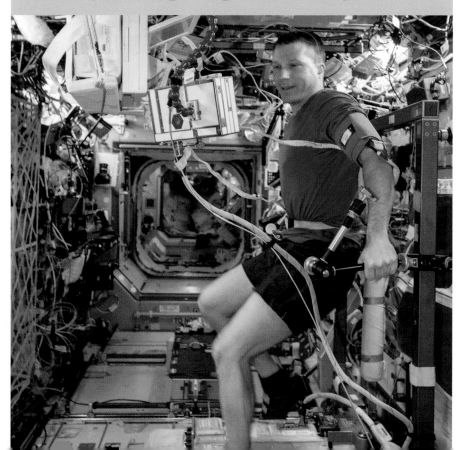

The ISS has several different laboratories.

Some astronauts do experiments with plants. Some study diseases. Others study how space affects the human body.

STATION SUPPLIES

Space stations need a lot of help to stay running. Solar panels make power. Spacecraft from Earth help, too. They carry supplies such as food and tools. They also transport astronauts.

CHAPTER 4

LOOKING AHEAD

In 2022, **NASA** said the ISS would last until 2030. Tiangong may last longer. Scientists planned to add more modules.

In July 2021, Russia added a new module to the ISS.

NASA planned to build a station that orbits the Moon. The station would help with future Moon landings.

FAST FACT

NASA named its lunar station Gateway.

NASA sent a tiny spacecraft to the Moon in 2022. It helped NASA figure out the lunar station's orbit.

Companies are also working on space stations. One company started missions to the ISS in 2022. The missions helped the company get ready for its own station.

SPACE TOURISM

Some companies let people pay to visit the ISS. They do experiments for a short time. Then they return to Earth. Scientists also hope to allow tourists to visit Tiangong.

Astronauts from the United States, Europe, Russia, and the private company Axiom posed for a photo on the ISS in 2022.

COMPREHENSION QUESTIONS

Write your answers on a separate piece of paper.

1. Write a paragraph about life on a space station.

2. Which space station would you most like to visit? Why?

3. What was the first modular space station?

    A. the International Space Station

    B. Mir

    C. Gateway

4. What would happen if astronauts did not exercise on space stations?

    A. Their bodies would be much weaker when they returned to Earth.

    B. Their bodies would be much stronger when they returned to Earth.

    C. They would get too bored on the space station.

5. What does **tethered** mean in this book?

*During spacewalks, astronauts are **tethered** to the space station. One end of a cable attaches to the astronaut. The other attaches to the station.*

    A. connected

    B. away from

    C. still inside

6. What does **transport** mean in this book?

*Spacecraft from Earth help, too. They carry supplies such as food and tools. They also **transport** astronauts.*

    A. to run out of supplies

    B. to fix something that is broken

    C. to bring from one place to another

Answer key on page 32.

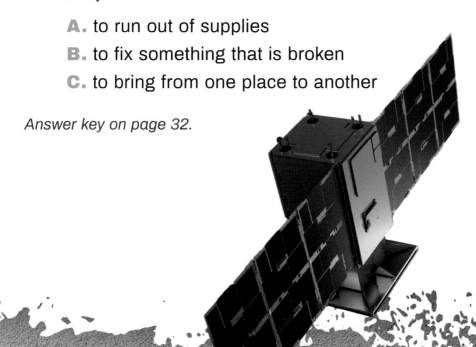

GLOSSARY

airlock
An area with two doors that lets astronauts move between a spacecraft and space.

docking ports
Areas where one spacecraft joins with another.

laboratories
Places where people study science, often by running tests.

modular
Made with different parts that connect together.

NASA
Short for National Aeronautics and Space Administration. NASA is the United States' space organization.

orbit
A curved path around an object in space.

Soviet Union
A country in Europe and Asia that existed from 1922 to 1991.

space station
A spacecraft where astronauts can live. It orbits a planet or moon.

TO LEARN MORE

BOOKS

Gagne, Tammy. *Space Tourism*. Lake Elmo, MN: Focus Readers, 2023.

Murray, Julie. *International Space Station*. Minneapolis: Abdo Publishing, 2019.

Olson, Elsie. *Spectacular Space Stations*. Minneapolis: Lerner Publications, 2020.

ONLINE RESOURCES

Visit **www.apexeditions.com** to find links and resources related to this title.

ABOUT THE AUTHOR

Dalton Rains is an author and editor from Saint Paul, Minnesota. He loves to learn about new science discoveries.

INDEX

ANSWER KEY:
1. Answers will vary; 2. Answers will vary; 3. B; 4. A; 5. A; 6. C